# CAT
## WILL RHYME WITH
# HAT

# CAT
## WILL RHYME WITH
# HAT

## A BOOK OF POEMS

Compiled by Jean Chapman

*Illustrated by Peter Parnall*

CHARLES SCRIBNER'S SONS
NEW YORK

Charles Scribner's Sons Books for Young Readers
Macmillan Publishing Company
866 Third Avenue, New York, NY 10022
Collier Macmillan Canada, Inc.

Printed in the United States of America
First Edition

10   9   8   7   6   5   4   3   2   1

Library of Congress Cataloging-in-Publication Data

Cat will rhyme with hat.
Includes indexes.
Summary: A collection of poems, (mostly)
celebrating the charm and behavior of cats.
1. Cats—Juvenile poetry.   2. Children's poetry.
[1. Cats—Poetry.   2. Poetry—Collections]
I. Chapman, Jean.   II. Parnall, Peter, ill.
PN6110.C3C37   1986       808.81'936       86-17817
ISBN 0-684-18747-7

## ACKNOWLEDGMENTS

The compiler and the publishers gratefully acknowledge the following
poets, publishers, and agents for permission to reprint poems in this
anthology. Every effort has been made to locate all persons having
any rights or interests in the material published here. If some acknowl-
edgments have not been made, their omission is unintentional and is
regretted.

"Cat Will Rhyme with Hat" by Spike Milligan, from UNSPUN SOCKS
FROM A CHICKEN'S LAUNDRY. Reprinted by permission of Michael
Joseph Ltd., in association with M. & J. Hobbs.

"The Kitten" by Ogden Nash, from VERSES FROM 1929 ON. Copyright
1940 by the Curtis Publishing Company. First appeared in *The Saturday
Evening Post.* Reprinted by permission of Little, Brown and Company and
by André Deutsch Ltd.

"A Kitten" by Eleanor Farjeon, from ELEANOR FARJEON'S POEMS
FOR CHILDREN (J.B. Lippincott). Copyright 1933, 1961 by Eleanor

*For Nancy W.*
*and*
*Clare C.*
*and*
*especially*
*you*

## *Cat Will Rhyme with Hat*

Cat will rhyme with Hat
But that my friend is all.
A Hat won't drink a bowl of milk
And you can't hang your Cat in the hall.

SPIKE MILLIGAN

# Contents

The Trouble with a Kitten 1

I Am the Cat 9

Cats Sleep Fat and Walk Thin 19

No One Knows What They Have in Mind 29

That's a Matter of Taste 35

Tip the Saucer of the Moon 41

Tough, Lean, and Scrawny 51

My Cat 61

*Indexes* 75

# The Trouble with a Kitten

## The Kitten

The trouble with a kitten is
THAT
Eventually it becomes a
CAT.

OGDEN NASH

## Nine Lives

My kitty cat has nine lives.
Yes, nine long lives has she.
Three to spend in eating,
Three to spend in sleeping
And three to spend up the chestnut tree.

TRADITIONAL

## A Kitten

He's nothing much but fur
And two round eyes of blue,
He has a giant purr
And a midget mew.

He darts and pats the air,
He starts and cocks his ear,
When there is nothing there
For him to see and hear.

He runs around in rings,
But why we cannot tell;
With sideways leaps he springs
At things invisible—

Then half-way through a leap
His startled eyeballs close,
And he drops off to sleep
With one paw on his nose.

ELEANOR FARJEON


## Kitty Cornered

Psst, psst.
Feel the kitten's silken fur
and hear her
soft as velvet
purr.

Softly, softly,
purr, purr, purr.
Purr, purrrrrrrrr.

Grrrrrr.
The kitten doesn't want to play,
not today,
Grr, grrr.

Psst, little kitten,
don't run away.
Let me stroke your fur.
Softly, softly,
purr, purr, purr.

Meow, not now,
Meow, meow,
MEOW,
*NOT NOWWWWWWWWWWWW!*

EVE MERRIAM

## *Kitty*

Look at pretty little kitty
Gnawing on a bone!
How I wish she'd eat some fish
And leave my leg alone.

DOUG MCLEOD

5

## The Kitten and the Falling Leaves

See the kitten on the wall,
Sporting with the leaves that fall,
Withered leaves—one, two and three—
From the lofty elder-tree!
Through the calm and frosty air
Of this morning bright and fair,
Eddying round and round they sink
Softly, slowly: one might think,
From the motions that are made,
Every little leaf conveyed
Sylph or Faery hither tending,
To this lower world descending,
Each invisible and mute,
In his wavering parachute.

But—the Kitten, how she starts,
Crouches, stretches paws, and darts!
First at one, and then its fellow
Just as light and just as yellow.
There are many now—now one—
Now they stop and there are none.

What intenseness of desire
In her upward eye of fire!
With a tiger-leap half way
Now she meets the coming prey,
Lets it go as fast, and then
Has it in her power again:
Now she works with three or four,

Like an Indian conjurer;
Quick as he in feats of art,
Far beyond in joy of heart.
Were her antics played in the eye
Of a thousand standers-by,
Clapping hands with shout and stare,
What would little Tabby care
For the plaudits of the crowd?

WILLIAM WORDSWORTH

## For a Dead Kitten

Put the rubber mouse away,
Pick the spools up from the floor,
What was velvet-shod, and gay,
Will not want them any more.

What was warm, is strangely cold.
Whence dissolved the little breath?
How could this small body hold
So immense a thing as Death?

SARA HENDERSON HAY

# I Am the Cat

## The Prayer of the Cat

Lord,
I am the cat.
It is not, exactly, that I have something to ask of You!
No—
I ask nothing of anyone—
but,
if You have by some chance, in some celestial barn,
a little white mouse
or a saucer of milk,
I know someone who would relish them.
Wouldn't You like someday
to put a curse on the whole race of dogs?
If so I should say,

Amen

CARMEN BERNOS DE GASZTOLD
*Translated by Rumer Godden*


## Catmint

Bear in mind
  Never to push a cat from behind;
  There is no humiliation for a cat
  Greater than that.

11

Cats are proud
And no familiarity is allowed.
    To a friend
They will condescend
And occasionally are seen
    To lean;
But they will not go out of their way
    To betray
Signs of affection
Or recollection
Nor will incline their ears
    To taunts or jeers.
At the least presentiment
    Of sentiment
They simply retire
    In ire.
Do not shout or call
That will not do at all.
Fish and milk
    And that ilk
May be used as easement
    And appeasement
But even mice
Do not entice
    The well-bred,
For the cat
    Is an aristocrat;
Get that into your head.

ERIC CLOUGH TAYLOR

## Terry

terry
my tabby-cat
daylong during winter
tattered ears hugged flat
creeps his wily head
closer and closer
to the heaped coal fire
till the flames
singe his fur
bake his belly


later
after I've appealed
to him vainly
to move when I want
to mend the fire
ignoring the names
I call him will yield
like a blob of mercury
to my touch
confident
I'd let him lie I'd rather
let the fire out


when each day
he steps out-
of-doors a bit longer
I know
spring is truly on her way

and when he quits
the house altogether
and sits
trimming and combing his
burnt beard I know
spring has arrived at last
the sun high
he goes to bask
on his back on the path
legs straight and wide
as if tied
bared claws curved to draw
the mouse-warm heat inside
till he begins to purr
and then snore

nap over
rises
lowers his head
stretches
heaps his lean belly
high on his back
becomes for a moment
dromedary
slackens back to cat
grins
licks his chops
flirts
a defiant tail
deliberately skirts
the border biting
off heads of flowers

14

never dead ones
always the brightest ones

he swaggers as he walks
pleased I'm watching
pleased I'm shaking
my rueful head

stalks slowly to the lilac tree
sits tall egyptian
tiered in leaf light
yearns for the moment when
young birds try their flight
and flutter from the bough
to where he waits below

ALBERT ROWE

I am the cat that walks by himself
And all places are alike to me.

RUDYARD KIPLING

## Cat

Sometimes I am an unseen
marmalade cat, the friendliest colour,
making off through a window without permission,
pacing along a broken-glass wall to the greenhouse,
jumping down with a soft, four-pawed thump,
finding two inches open of the creaking door
with the loose brass handle,
slipping impossibly in,
flattening my fur at the hush and touch of the sudden
    warm air,
avoiding the tiled gutter of slow green water,
skirting the potted nests of tetchy cactuses,
and sitting with my tail flicked
skilfully underneath me, to sniff
the azaleas   the azaleas   the azaleas.

ALAN BROWNJOHN


God created Cat and asked,
"From whom will you receive your daily bread?"

And Cat answered God,
"An absent-minded woman who does not remember
to latch tight her kitchen door."

TRADITIONAL ISRAELI

## Cat

The fat cat on the mat
    may seem to dream
of nice mice that suffice
    for him, or cream;
but he free, maybe,
    walks in thought
unbowed, proud, where loud
    roared and fought
his kin, lean and slim,
    or deep in den
in the East feasted on beasts
    and tender men.

The giant lion with iron
    claw in paw,
and huge ruthless tooth
    in gory jaw;
the pard dark-starred,
    fleet upon feet,
that oft soft from aloft
    leaps on his meat
where woods loom in gloom—
    far now they be,
    fierce and free,
    and tamed is he;
but fat cat on the mat
    kept as a pet,
    he does not forget.

J. R. R. TOLKIEN

# Cats Sleep Fat
# and Walk Thin

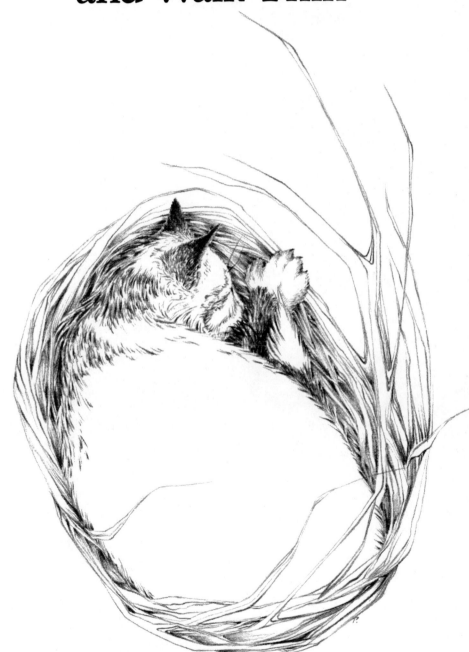

## Catalogue

Cats sleep fat and walk thin.
Cats, when they sleep, slump;
When they wake, stretch and begin
Over, pulling their ribs in.
Cats walk thin.

Cats wait in a lump,
Jump in a streak.
Cats, when they jump, are sleek
As a grape slipping its skin—
They have technique.
Oh, cats don't creak.
They sneak.

Cats sleep fat.
They spread out comfort underneath them
Like a good mat,
As if they picked the place
And then sat;
You walk around one
As if he were the City Hall
After that.

If male,
A cat is apt to sing on a major scale;
This concert is for everybody, this
Is wholesale.
For a baton, he wields a tail.

(He is also found,
When happy, to resound
With an enclosed and private sound.)

A cat condenses.
He pulls in his tail to go under bridges,
And himself go under fences.
Cats fit
In any size box or kit,
And if a large pumpkin grew under one,
He could arch over it.

When everyone else is just ready to go out,
The cat is just ready to come in.
He's not where he's been.
Cats sleep fat and walk thin.

ROSALIE MOORE


## Double Dutch

That crafty cat, a buff-black Siamese,
Sniffing through wild wood, sagely, silently goes—
Prick ears, lank legs, alertly twitching nose—
And on her secret errand reads with ease
A language no man knows.

WALTER DE LA MARE

## Cat

My cat
Is quiet.
She moves without a sound.
Sometimes she stretches herself curving
On tiptoe.
Sometimes she crouches low
And creeping.

Sometimes she rubs herself against a chair,
And there
   With a *miew* and a *miew*
   And a purrrr     purrrr     purrrr
   She curls up
   And goes to sleep.

My cat
Lives through a black hole
Under the house.
So one day I
Crawled in after her.
And it was dark
And I sat
And didn't know
Where to go.
And then—

Two yellow-white
Round little lights
came moving . . . moving . . . toward me.
And there

With a *miew* and a *miew*
  And a purrrr     purrrr     purrrr
My cat
Rubbed, soft, against me.

  And I knew
  The lights
  Were MY CAT'S EYES
  In the dark.

DOROTHY BARUCH

## White Cat in Moonlight

Through moonlight's milk
She slowly passes
As soft as silk
Between tall grasses.
I watch her go
So sleek, so white
As white as snow.
The moon so bright
I hardly know
White moon, white fur,
Which is the light
And which is her.

DOUGLAS GIBSON

## Midwife Cat

Beyond the fence she hesitates,
   And drops a paw, and tries the dust.
It is clearing, but she waits
   No longer minute than she must.

Though a dozen foes may dart
   From out the grass, she crouches by,
Then runs to where the silos start
   To heave their shadows far and high.

Here she folds herself and sleeps;
   But in a moment she has put
The dreams aside; and now she creeps
   Across the open, foot by foot.

Till at the threshold of a shed
   She smells the water and the corn
Where a sow is on her bed
   And little pigs are being born.

Silently she leaps, and walks
   All night upon a narrow rafter,
Whence at intervals she talks
   Wise to them she watches after.

MARK VAN DOREN

## Cat

The black cat yawns,
Opens her jaws,
Stretches her legs,
And shows her claws.

Then she gets up
And stands on four
Long stiff legs
And yawns some more.

She shows her sharp teeth,
She stretches her lip,
Her slice of a tongue
Turns up at the tip.

Lifting herself
On her delicate toes,
She arches her back
As high as it goes.

She lets herself down
With particular care,
And pads away
With her tail in the air.

MARY BRITTON MILLER

26

## Circle Sleeper

The cat curls in a whorl
like the shell of a snail,
her black patent nose
snugly warmed by her tail.

Her coat freshly washed,
wire whiskers pressed flat,
she sinks in the rug,
a black puddle of cat.

JEAN H. MARVIN

# No One Knows
# What They Have in Mind

## My Cat Mrs. Lick-a-chin

Some of the cats I know about
Spend a lot of time in and a lot of time out.
Or a lot of time out and a little time in.
But my cat, Mrs. Lick-a-chin
Never knows *where* she wants to go.

If I let her in she looks at me
And begins to sing that she wants to go out
So I open the door and she looks about
And begins to sing, "Please let me in!"
Poor silly Mrs. Lick-a-chin!

The thing about cats, as you may find
Is that no one knows what they have in mind.
And I'll tell you something about that
No one knows it less than my cat.

JOHN CIARDI

## The Cat

One gets a wife, one gets a house,
Eventually one gets a mouse.
One gets some words regarding mice,
One gets a kitty in a trice.
By two a.m., or thereabout,

31

The mouse is in, the cat is out.
It dawns upon one, in one's cot,
The mouse is still, the cat is not.
Instead of Pussy, says one's spouse,
One should have bought another mouse.

OGDEN NASH

## *That Cat*

The cat that comes to my window sill
When the moon looks cold and the night is still—
He comes in a frenzied state alone
With a tail that stands like a pine tree cone,
And says, "I have finished my evening lark,
And I think I can hear a hound dog bark.
My whiskers are frozen stuck to my chin.
I do wish you'd git up and let me in."
    That cat gits in.

But if in solitude of the night
He doesn't appear to be feeling right,
And rises and stretches and seeks the floor,
And some remote corner he would explore,
And doesn't feel satisfied just because
There's no good spot for to sharpen his claws,
And meows and canters uneasy about
Beyond the least shadow of any doubt
    That cat gits out.

BEN KING

## Pets

A dark November night. Late. The back door wide.
Beyond the doorway, the step off into space.
On the threshold, looking out,
With foxy furry tail lifted, a kitten.
Somewhere out there a badger, our lodger,
A stripe-faced rusher at cats, a grim savager,
Is crunching the bones and meat of a hare
That I left out for her twilight emergence
From under the outhouses.
The kitten flirts its tail, arches its back,
All its hairs are inquisitive.
Dare I go for a pee?
Something is moving there—just in dark.
A prowling lump. A tabby Tom. Grows.
And the battered master of the house
After a month at sea, comes through the doorway,
Recovered from his nearly fatal mauling,
Two probably three pounds heavier
Since that last appearance
When he brought in his remains to die or be doctored.
He deigns to recognize me,
With his criminal eyes, his deformed voice.
Then poises, head lowered, muscle-bound,
Like a bull for the judges,
A thick Devon bull,
Sniffing the celebration of sardines.

TED HUGHES

## A Different Door

When rain falls gray and unabating
And long kept in he stares out waiting
And no one heeds and starts unlatching
Our back door, Tom tries front-door scratching.

That cat, he's not what I'd call bright,
But for a chance—oh, even slight—
Of sunlit skies a lark might soar,
Who wouldn't scratch a different door?

X. J. KENNEDY

# That's a
# Matter of Taste

## Cat's Menu

I eat what I wish—
That's a matter of taste.
Whether liver or fish,
I eat what I wish.
Putting scraps in my dish
Is a terrible waste.
I eat what I wish—
It's a matter of taste.

WINIFRED CRAWFORD

## In Honour of Taffy Topaz

Taffy, the topaz-coloured cat,
Thinks now of this and now of that,
But chiefly of his meals.
Asparagus, and cream, and fish,
Are objects of his Freudian wish;
What you don't give, he steals.

His gallant heart is strongly stirred
By clink of plate or flight of bird,
He has a plumy tail;
At night he treads on stealthy pad
As merry as Sir Galahad
A-seeking of the Grail.

37

His amiable amber eyes
Are very friendly, very wise;
Like Buddha, grave and fat,
He sits, regardless of applause
And thinking, as he kneads his paws,
What fun to be a cat!

CHRISTOPHER MORLEY


## Montague Michael

Montague Michael
You're much too fat,
You wicked old, wily old,
Well-fed cat.

All night you sleep
On a cushion of silk,
And twice a day
I bring you milk.

And once in a while,
When you catch a mouse,
You're the proudest person
In all the house.

But spoilt as you are,
I tell you, cat,
This chair is all mine
And you can't have that!

ANONYMOUS

38

## Pussy, Pussy Baudrons

"Pussy, pussy baudrons
Where have you been?"

"I've been to London,
To see the Queen!"

"Pussy, pussy baudrons,
What got you there?"

"I got a good fat mousikie,
Running up the stair."

SCOTTISH NURSERY RHYME


## Under the Table Manners

It's very hard to be polite
    If you're a cat.
When other folk are up at the table
Eating all that they are able
    You are down on the mat
    If you're a cat.

You're expected just to sit
    If you're a cat,
Not to let them know you're there
By scratching at the chair
    Or with light respectful pat
    If you're a cat.

You are not to make a fuss
  If you're a cat.
Tho' there's fish upon the plate
You're expected just to wait,
  Wait prettily on the mat
  If you're a cat.

UNKNOWN

## The Fisherman's Hands

The fisherman's hands
are gnarled and worn
from wind and waves
while mine stay warm
inside my gloves.

"Why not wear gloves?"
I ask one day
when the wind is wild
and he bends to say
"Well, listen, child,

Have you ever known cats
Have you ever known kittens
that could catch mice
while wearing mittens?"

NANINE VALEN

40

# Tip the Saucer
of the Moon

## The Stray

The Cat, who sleeps upon the mat,
  Is not domestic as she seems:
From Amazon to Ararat,
  She prowls in her majestic dreams.
Each Alley Cat has power to stray
  In sleep, from dusty afternoon,
To pad along the Milky Way,
  and tip the saucer of the moon.

And, whosoever killed the Cat,
  Was not dull Care, as some declare—
She roams—the world's Immortal Stray—
  From Babylon to Finisterre.
And when, in sunny sitting-room,
  We see her sleep, with paws a-twitch,
She's clinging to a flying broom
  Behind a sleeping witch.

BARBARA EUPHAN TODD

## On a Night of Snow

Cat, if you go outdoors you must walk in the snow.
You will come back with little white shoes on your feet,
Little white slippers of snow that have heels of sleet.
Stay by the fire, my cat. Lie still, do not go.

See how the flames are leaping and hissing low;
I will bring you a saucer of milk like a marguerite,
So white and so smooth, so spherical and so sweet—
Stay with me, Cat. Outdoors the wild winds blow.

Outdoors the wild winds blow, Mistress, and dark is the
    night,
Strange voices cry in the trees, intoning strange lore;
And more than cats move, lit by our eyes' green light,
On silent feet where the meadow grasses hang hoar—
Mistress, there are portents abroad of magic and might
And things that are yet to be done. Open the door!

ELIZABETH COATSWORTH


## Moon

I have a white cat whose name is Moon;
He eats catfish from a wooden spoon,
And sleeps till five each afternoon.

Moon goes out when the moon is bright
And sycamore trees are spotted white
To sit and stare in the dead of night.

Beyond still water cries a loon,
Through mulberry leaves peers a wild baboon
And in Moon's eyes I see the moon.

WILLIAM JAY SMITH

## Wanted—A Witch's Cat

Wanted—a witch's cat.
Must have vigor and spite,
Be expert at hissing,
And good for a fight,
And have balance and poise
On a broomstick at night.

Wanted—a witch's cat.
Must have hypnotic eyes
To tantalise victims
And mesmerise spies,
And be an adept
At scanning skies.

Wanted—a witch's cat,
With a sly cunning smile,
A knowledge of spells
And a good deal of guile,
With a fairly hot temper
And plenty of bile.

Wanted—a witch's cat,
Who's not afraid to fly.
For a cat with strong nerves
The salary's high.
Wanted—a witch's cat;
Only the best need apply.

SHELAGH MCGEE

45

## Oh, Lovely, Lovely, Lovely!

The witch flew out on Hallowe'en,
Her hair was blue, her nose was green,
Her teeth the longest ever seen,
Oh, she was lovely, lovely, lovely!

Her cat was black and fit and fat,
He lashed his tail and humped his back,
He scritched and scratched and hissed and spat,
Oh, he was lovely, lovely, lovely!

They rode a cleaner, not a broom.
"Go left!" screeched Puss and spoke their doom.
She turned right—they hit the moon.
Oh, it was lovely, lovely, lovely.

ANONYMOUS

## The Cat

Within that porch, across the way,
I see two naked eyes this night;
Two eyes that neither shut nor blink,
Searching my face with a green light.

But cats to me are strange, so strange—
I cannot sleep if one is near;
And though I'm sure I see those eyes,
I'm not so sure a body's there!

W. H. DAVIES

## Gobbolino, the Witch's Cat

One fine night in a witch's cavern,
Two little kittens rolled on the floor;
One, called Sootica, was black all over:
The other, Gobbolino, had one white paw.
Who'll give a home to a kitten?
Who'll give a home to a cat?
Gobbolino you may call me,
I want just a fire and a mat.

One white paw and a sheen of tabby,
Two lovely eyes, not green, but blue.
None of the witches would take this kitten . . .
And neither did his mother know what to do.
Who'll give a home to a kitten?
Who'll give a home to a cat?
Gobbolino you may call me,
I want just a fire and a mat.

Then one day, when the sun was shining,
Gobbolino found he was all alone.
The witch had gone and deserted him for ever,
So Gobbolino washed himself, then he left home.
Who'll give a home to a kitten?
Who'll give a home to a cat?
Gobbolino you may call me,
I want just a fire and a mat.

G. C. WESTCOTT

## The Cat and the Moon

The cat went here and there
And the moon spun round like a top,
And the nearest kin of the moon,
The creeping cat, looked up.
Black Minnaloushe stared at the moon,
For, wander and wail as he would,
The pure cold light of the sky
Troubled his animal blood.
Minnaloushe runs in the grass
Lifting his delicate feet.
Do you dance, Minnaloushe, do you dance?
When two close kindred meet,
What better than call a dance?
Maybe the moon may learn,
Tired of that courtly fashion,
A new dance turn.
Minnaloushe creeps through the grass
From moonlit place to place,
The sacred moon overhead
Has taken a new phase.
Does Minnaloushe know that his pupils
Will pass from change to change,
And that from round to crescent,
From crescent to round they range?
Minnaloushe creeps through the grass
Alone, important and wise,
And lifts to the changing moon
His changing eyes.

W. B. YEATS

## Of Calico Cats

Wide awake and dreaming
of calico cats,
faces white and ginger,
black and ginger,
the faces of calico cats.

You stole my glance
as I watched,
and stared at the calico cats
in the moonlight;
and under a streetlamp
I saw you standing,
standing with calico cats.

The white is ginger,
ginger is black:
orange streetlights
cast their changeful glow.
The cats-eyes in the road
are gleaming,
and I am dreaming,
and cats are screaming,
the screams of calico cats.

KIRSTY SEYMOUR-URE

# Tough, Lean, and Scrawny

## Mister Alley Cat

When darkness comes to city streets
Mister Alley Cat sneaks out,
A mean old
Mangy old
Tough, lean and scrawny old
Alley Cat.
He's a flicker of fur in the lamplight
A shadow slinking past doors.
He's a bump and a howl about midnight,
A robber on velvet-soft paws.

His best evening coat is black, white and patchy
But he's quick on the draw with claws long and
     scratchy.
He's the toughest old tiger in a brawl or a fight
And many a cat has felt his sharp bite.

He plays King of the Castle on garbage tin lids.
He's Boss of the Pack—a real top cat
Who spells sudden death
For old Smelly the Rat.

That mean old
Mangy old
Tough, lean and scrawny old
Alley Cat.

JOHN MCGOWAN

## Macavity: The Mystery Cat

Macavity's a Mystery Cat: He's called the Hidden
     Paw—
For he's the master criminal who can defy the Law.
He's the bafflement of Scotland Yard, the Flying
     Squad's despair:
For when they reach the scene of crime—
     *Macavity's not there!*

Macavity, Macavity, there's no one like Macavity,
He's broken every human law, he breaks the law
     of gravity.
His powers of levitation would make a fakir stare,
And when you reach the scene of crime—
     *Macavity's not there!*
You may seek him in the basement, you may look
     up in the air—
But I tell you at once and once again, *Macavity's
     not there!*

Macavity's a ginger cat, he's very tall and thin;
You would know him if you saw him, for his eyes
     are sunken in.
His brow is deeply lined with thought, his head is
     highly domed;
His coat is dusty from neglect, his whiskers are
     uncombed.
He sways his head from side to side, with
     movements like a snake;
And when you think he's half asleep, he's always
     wide awake.

Macavity, Macavity, there's no one like Macavity,
For he's a fiend in feline shape, a monster of
    depravity.
You may meet him in a by-street, you may see him
    in the square—
But when a crime's discovered, then *Macavity's not
there!*

He's outwardly respectable. (They say he cheats at
    cards.)
And his footprints are not found in any file of
    Scotland Yard's.
And when the larder's looted, or the jewel-case is
    rifled,
Or when the milk is missing, or another Peke's
    been stifled,
Or the greenhouse glass is broken, and the trellis
    past repair—
Ay, there's the wonder of the thing! *Macavity's not
there!*

And when the Foreign Office find a Treaty's gone
    astray,
Or the Admiralty lose some plans and drawings by
    the way,
There may be a scrap of paper in the hall or on
    the stair—
But it's useless to investigate—*Macavity's not there!*
And when the loss has been disclosed, the Secret
    Service say:
"It *must* have been *Macavity*"—but he's a mile
    away.

55

You'll be sure to find him resting, or a-licking of
    his thumbs,
Or engaged in doing complicated long division
    sums.

Macavity, Macavity, there's no one like Macavity,
There never was a Cat of such deceitfulness and
    suavity.
He always has an alibi, and one or two to spare:
At whatever time the deed took place—
    MACAVITY WASN'T THERE!
And they say that all the Cats whose wicked deeds
    are widely known,
(I might mention Mungojerrie, I might mention
    Griddlebone)
Are nothing more than agents for the Cat who all
    the time
Just controls their operations: the Napoleon of
    Crime!

T. S. ELIOT

## The Cat Came Back

Now Mister Johnson had troubles of his own,
He had an old yellow cat that wouldn't leave its home.
He tried ev'rything he knew to keep the cat away.
He took it up to Canada and told it for to stay
But the cat came back the very next day,
The old cat came back.
Thought he was a gonner,
The cat came back, cause he couldn't stay.

He gave the boy a dollar for to set the cat afloat,
He took him up the river in a sack in a boat.
Well the fishing it was fun 'til the news got around
That the boat is missing and the boy was drowned.
But the cat came back the very next day,
The old cat came back.
Thought he was a gonner,
The cat came back, cause he couldn't stay.


On the telegraph wire the birds were sitting in a
    bunch,
He saw six or seven, said, he'd have 'em for his lunch,
He climbed softly to the top and put his foot upon
    the wire,
Well his tail was scorched off and his tail caught fire.
But the cat came back the very next day,
The old cat came back.
Thought he was a gonner,
The cat came back, cause he couldn't stay.


Well they threw him in the kennel when the dog was
    asleep
And the bones of cats lay piled in a heap.
Well the kennel burst apart and the dog flew out the
    side
With his ears chewed off and holes in his hide.
But the cat came back the very next day,
The old cat came back.
Thought he was a gonner,
The cat came back, cause he couldn't stay.

AMERICAN TRADITIONAL

## The Wild Cat

The wildcat sits on the rocks.
His hair is spitting fire
into the morning air.
His eyes are yellow.

Club-headed dynamic cat,
he is all power and force.
Among the dry green grass,
the hares are playing.

The air is clear and pure.
The hares are leaping and jumping
over invisible fences
of pure brilliant blue.

The wildcat sits by himself
on his stony throne, not thinking.
His fur simmers like fire
snarling and sparkling.

IAIN CRICHTON SMITH

## Country Barnyard

Cats and kittens, kittens and cats
under the barn and under the shed;
a face by the steps, a tail by the ramp
and off they go, if they hear a tread!

Sleep in the sun with one eye on guard,
doze in the grass with a listening ear,
run for the darkness under the barn
as soon as a human being draws near!

Not quite wild and not quite tame,
thin and limber, with hungry eye:
the house cat sits at the kitchen door
disdainfully watching her kin go by.

ELIZABETH COATSWORTH

## Five Eyes

In Hans' old mill his three black cats
Watch the bins for the thieving rats.
Whisker and claw, they crouch in the night,
Their five eyes smouldering green and bright:
Squeaks from the flour-sacks, squeaks from where
The cold wind stirs on the empty stair,
Squeaking and scampering everywhere.
Then down they pounce, now in, now out,
At whisking tail, and sniffing snout;
While lean old Hans he snores away
Till peep of light at break of day;
Then up he climbs to his creaking mill,
Out come his cats all grey with meal—
Jekkel, and Jessup, and one-eyed Jill.

WALTER DE LA MARE

## The Kilkenny Cats

There wanst was two cats in Kilkenny.
Each thought there was one cat too many.
So they quarrel'd and fit,
They scratched and they bit,
Till, excepting their nails,
And the tips of their tails,
Instead of two cats, there warnt any.

TRADITIONAL

# My Cat

## Pangur Ban

I and Pangur Ban, my cat,
'Tis a like task we are at;
Hunting mice is his delight,
Hunting words I sit all night.

Better far than praise of men
'Tis to sit with book and pen;
Pangur bears me no ill-will,
He too plies his simple skill.

'Tis a merry thing to see
At our tasks how glad are we,
When at home we sit and find
Entertainment to our mind.

Oftentimes a mouse will stray
In the hero Pangur's way;
Oftentimes my keen thought set
Takes a meaning in its net.

'Gainst the wall he sets his eye
Full and fierce and sharp and sly;
'Gainst the wall of knowledge I
All my little wisdom try.

When a mouse darts from its
    den,
O how glad is Pangur then!

O what gladness do I prove
When I solve the doubts of love!

So in peace our tasks we ply,
Pangur Ban, my cat, and I;
In our arts we find our bliss,
I have mine and he has his.

Practice every day has made
Pangur perfect in his trade;
I get wisdom day and night
Turning darkness into light.

UNKNOWN STUDENT
*Monastery of Carintha*
*eighth century*
*Gaelic translated by Dr. Robin Flower*


## The Singing Cat

It was a little captive cat
   Upon a crowded train
His mistress takes him from his box
   To ease his fretful pain.

She holds him tight upon her knee
   The graceful animal
And all the people look at him
   He is so beautiful.

But oh he pricks and oh he prods
   And turns upon her knee

Then lifteth up his innocent voice
   In plaintive melody.

He lifteth up his innocent voice
   He lifteth up, he singeth
And to each human countenance
   A smile of grace he bringeth.

He lifteth up his innocent paw
   Upon her breast he clingeth
And everybody cries, Behold
   The cat, the cat that singeth.

He lifteth up his innocent voice
   He lifteth up, he singeth
And all the people warm themselves
   In the love his beauty bringeth.

STEVIE SMITH


## Fourteen Ways of Touching Peter

### I

You can push
your thumb
in the
ridge
between his
shoulder-blades
to please him

### II

Starting
at its root,
you can let
his whole
tail
flow
through your hand.

III
Forming
a fist
you can let
him rub
his bone
skull
against it, hard. ·

IV
When he makes
bread,
you can lift
him
by his under-
sides on your
knuckles.

V
In hot
weather
you can itch
the fur
under
his chin. He
likes that.

VI
At night
you can hoist
him
out of his bean-stalk,
sleepily
clutching
paper bags.

VII
Pressing
his head against
your cheek,
you can carry
him
in the dark
safely.

VIII
In late autumn
you can find
seeds
adhering
to his fur.
They are
plenty.

## IX

You can prise
his jaws
open,
helping
any medicine
he won't
abide, go down.

## X

You can touch
his
feet, only
if
he is relaxed.
He
doesn't like it.

## XI

You can comb
spare thin
fur
from his coat,
so he won't
get
fur-ball.

## XII

You can shake
his rigid
chicken-leg leg,
scouring his
hind-quarters
with his Vim
tongue.

## XIII

Dumping
hot fish
on his plate, you can
fend
him off,
pushing
and purring.

## XIV

You can have
him shrimp
along you,
breathing
whenever
you want
to compose poems.

GEORGE MACBETH

67

## Elegy for Delina

Inevitable, of course. Very old now, she
Ate little food and couldn't keep it down,
Grew thin and sad. Gentle, gentle, though,
And loving as ever, a frown
Enough to check her. Upon my knee,
Assent given at a glance from her,
Climbed still and clawed and turned,
My flinching ignored—she never learned—
Settled, familiar, to purr herself to sleep,
My fingers quiet on her fur.

A little cat, she had, none like her,
A sweet and varied voice. Forgive the foolishness,
I was sure she talked, asked to come and go,
Constantly caught my eye, answering
(I was so fond of her) all my meaningless
Endearments with her tiny tender cry,
Subtle-toned, responsive to my feeling.
I treasured it as talking with a friend.

Would walk, murmurous, tail carried high,
From room to room with me, and when
I went to write would on my table spring
And plump down on the very book
I wanted to use next. Pushed gently
Away she with reproachful look
Would find, incredible, a space to lie
Uneven against corners, content to be with me.

It was right to put her down, and I believed
I'd not much miss her. To find myself aggrieved,
My own life less, its corners closer crowded.
Twelve years of fondness can't be ended so.
I think of its beginning, mind holding her,
See the bright kitten newly carried home,
Climb, quicksilver grey, up the curtain's height,
I applauding . . .
        At her fancied call tonight,
Forgetful I rise, open the door, to let in
Only the sad and alien-angled light.

ALBERT ROWE


## Cat

My cat has got no name,
We simply call him Cat.
He doesn't seem to blame
Anyone for that.

For he is not like us
Who often, I'm afraid,
Kick up quite a fuss
If *our* names are mislaid.

As if, without a name,
We'd be no longer there
But like a tiny flame
Vanish in bright air.

My pet, he doesn't care
About such things as that:
Black buzz and golden stare
Require no name but Cat.

VERNON SCANNELL

## The Little Cat

Four Irish scholars went
to sea for the Love of God,
and took nothing with them,
only the youngest said,
"I think I will take
the little cat."

*Translated from Medieval Latin*
*by Helen Waddell*

## If I Lost My Little Cat

If I lost my little cat, I should be sad without it,
I should ask St. Jerome what to do about it,
I should ask St. Jerome, just because of that
He's the only saint I know that kept a pussy cat.

TRADITIONAL ENGLISH NURSERY RHYME

## Territory

My cat
lives next door.
When they go to work
he comes, paw by paw,
to share my sun,
and wash his face
to show all cats
that
he is in his daily place
and I am his.

JEAN CHAPMAN

## Epitaph for a Persian Kitten

Death, who one day taketh all,
Wise or good or great or small,
Every creature of the air,
Every creature of the sea,
All life here and everywhere,
What is thine we give to thee
Neither great nor very wise,
Yet beloved in our eyes,
   Lightly hold and gently keep
   A small good kitten in her sleep.

MIRIAM VEDDER

71

## My Old Cat

My old cat is dead,
Who would butt me with his head.
He had the sleekest fur.
He had the blackest purr.
Always gentle with us
Was this black puss,
But when I found him today
Stiff and cold where he lay
His look was a lion's,
Full of rage, defiance:
Oh, he would not pretend
That what came was a friend
But met it in pure hate.
Well died, my old cat.

HAL SUMMERS

## The Lost Cat

She took a last and simple meal when there were
        none to see her steal—
    A jug of cream upon the shelf, a fish prepared
        for dinner;
And now she walks a distant street with delicately
        sandalled feet,
    And no one gives her much to eat or weeps to see
        her thinner.

O my beloved come again, come back in joy, come
     back in pain,
    To end our searching with a mew, or with a purr
     our grieving;
And you shall have for lunch or tea whatever fish
     swim in the sea
    And all the cream that's meant for me—and not
     a word of thieving!

E. V. RIEU

## A Home Without a Cat

A home without a cat, and a well-fed,
well petted and properly revered cat,
may be a perfect home, *perhaps,* but
how can it prove its title?

MARK TWAIN

# Title Index

Calico Cats, Of, 49
Cat, 16
Cat, 17
Cat, 23–24
Cat, 26
Cat, 69–70
Catalogue, 21–22
Cat and the Moon, The, 48
Cat Came Back, The, 56–57
Catmint, 11–12
Cat's Menu, 37
Cat, That, 32
Cat, The, 31–32
Cat, The, 46
Cat Will Rhyme with Hat, ix
Circle Sleeper, 27
Country Barnyard, 58–59

Different Door, A, 34
Double Dutch, 22

Elegy for Delina, 68–69
Epitaph for a Persian Kitten, 71

Fisherman's Hands, The, 40
Five Eyes, 59
For a Dead Kitten, 7
Fourteen Ways of Touching Peter, 65–67

Gobbolino, the Witch's Cat, 47
God created Cat and asked, 16

Home Without a Cat, A, 73
Honour of Taffy Topaz, In, 37–38

I am the cat that walks by himself, 15
If I Lost My Little Cat, 70

Kilkenny Cats, The, 60
Kitten, A, 4
Kitten and the Falling Leaves, The, 6–7
Kitten, The, 3
Kitty, 5
Kitty Cornered, 4–5

Little Cat, The, 70
Lost Cat, The, 72–73

Macavity: The Mystery Cat, 54–56
Midwife Cat, 25
Mister Alley Cat, 53
Montague Michael, 38
Moon, 44
My Cat Mrs. Lick-a-chin, 31
My Old Cat, 72

Night of Snow, On a, 43–44
Nine Lives, 3

Oh, Lovely, Lovely, Lovely!, 46

Pangur Ban, 63–64
Pets, 33
Prayer of the Cat, The, 11
Pussy, Pussy Baudrons, 39

Singing Cat, The, 64–65
Stray, The, 43

Territory, 71
Terry, 13-15

Under the Table Manners,
   39–40

Wanted—A Witch's Cat, 45
Wild Cat, The, 58
White Cat in Moonlight, 24

# Author Index

Baruch, Dorothy, 23–24
Brownjohn, Alan, 16

Chapman, Jean, 71

Ciardi, John, 31
Coatsworth, Elizabeth, 43–44, 58–59
Crawford, Winifred, 37

Davies, W.H., 46
de la Mare, Walter, 22, 59
de Gasztold, Carmen Bernos, 11

Eliot, T.S., 54–56

Farjeon, Eleanor, 4
Flower, Robin (translator), 64

Gibson, Douglas, 24
Godden, Rumer (translator), 11

Hay, Sara Henderson, 7
Hughes, Ted, 33

Kennedy, X.J., 34
King, Ben, 32
Kipling, Rudyard, 15

MacBeth, George, 65–67
Marvin, Jean H., 27
McGee, Shelagh, 45
McGowan, John, 53

McLeod, Doug, 5
Merriam, Eve, 4–5
Miller, Mary Britton, 26
Milligan, Spike, ix
Moore, Rosalie, 21–22
Morley, Christopher, 37–38

Nash, Ogden, 3, 31–32

Rieu, E.V., 72–73
Rowe, Albert, 13–15, 68–69

Scannell, Vernon, 69–70
Seymour-Ure, Kirsty, 49
Smith, Iain Crichton, 58
Smith, Stevie, 64–65
Smith, William Jay, 44
Summers, Hal, 72

Taylor, Eric Clough, 11–12
Todd, Barbara Euphan, 43
Tolkien, J.R.R., 17
Twain, Mark, 73

Valen, Nanine, 40
van Doren, Mark, 25
Vedder, Miriam, 71

Waddell, Helen (translator), 70
Westcott, G.C., 47
Wordsworth, William, 6–7

Yeats, W.B., 48

# First Line Index

A dark November night. Late. The back door wide, 33
A home without a cat, and a well-fed, 73

Bear in mind, 11
Beyond the fence she hesitates, 25

Cat, if you go outdoors you must walk in the snow, 43
Cats and kittens, kittens and cats, 58
Cats sleep fat and walk thin, 21
Cat will rhyme with Hat, ix

Death, who one day taketh all, 71

Four Irish scholars went, 70

God created Cat and asked, 16

He's nothing much but fur, 4

I am the cat that walks by himself, 15
I and Pangur Ban, my cat, 63
I eat what I wish—, 37
If I lost my little cat, I should be sad without it, 70
I have a white cat whose name is Moon, 44
Inevitable, of course. Very old now, she, 68
In Hans' old mill his three black cats, 59
It's very hard to be polite, 39
It was a little captive cat, 64

Look at pretty little kitty, 5
Lord, 11

Macavity's a Mystery Cat: He's called the Hidden Paw—, 54
Montague Michael, 38

My cat, 23
My cat, 71
My cat has got no name, 69
My kitty cat has nine lives, 3
My old cat is dead, 72

Now Mister Johnson had troubles of his own, 56

One fine night in a witch's cavern, 47
One gets a wife, one gets a house, 31

Psst, psst, 4
"Pussy, pussy baudrons," 39
Put the rubber mouse away, 7

See the kitten on the wall, 6
She took a last and simple meal when there were none to see her
    steal—, 72
Some of the cats I know about, 31
Sometimes I am an unseen, 16

Taffy, the topaz-coloured cat, 37
terry, 13
That crafty cat, a buff-black Siamese, 22
The black cat yawns, 26
The cat curls in a whorl, 27
The cat that comes to my window sill, 32
The cat went here and there, 48
The Cat, who sleeps upon the mat, 43
The fat cat on the mat, 17
The fisherman's hands, 40
There wanst was two cats in Kilkenny, 60
The trouble with a kitten is, 3
The wildcat sits on the rocks, 58
The witch flew out on Hallowe'en, 46
Through moonlight's milk, 24

Wanted—a witch's cat, 45
When darkness comes to city streets, 53
When rain falls gray and unabating, 34
Wide awake and dreaming, 49
Within that porch, across the way, 46

You can push, 65